LIFE
IT'S MORE THAN JUST
WORDS

LIFE
IT'S MORE THAN JUST
WORDS

Mama Syl'V

authorHOUSE®

AuthorHouse™ LLC
1663 Liberty Drive
Bloomington, IN 47403
www.authorhouse.com
Phone: 1-800-839-8640

Published by AuthorHouse   07/22/2013

ISBN: 978-1-4817-7411-6 (sc)
ISBN: 978-1-4817-7410-9 (e)

Library of Congress Control Number: 2013912274

Dedication

This book is dedicated to the memory of Anderson and Velmer Freeman, who brought me into their lives at four months and twenty-three days old, who nurtured me and gave me a cherished childhood experience and a wonderful upbringing, to my Auntie, Rosetta Mitchell, who always supported and believed in me, and to my cousin, LaVerne Kennedy, who has been my confidant and my friend. A note of thanks to Nicole Mayrant, who helped me complete this task. Your care and support means so much. A special I love you to Fredricka Mattison and Joyce Frink.

To my ever-loving son, Vaughn, you made motherhood a delightful adventure.

I love you much!

Everyone has a story to tell

Contents

Family Life

Life in The World

Life's Drama

Home

Someone said . . . home is where your heart is . . . it
could be!
Home is where you build family ties . . . it has to be!
Home is where you find peace and joy . . . it's gotta be!
Home is your safe haven, to relax and rest in
security . . . it must be!
Home is your space, your special place to be you . . .
it needs to be!
Home is where you are introduced to love . . . it ought
to be!
Home is where you can collect your thoughts and
dream your desires . . . it can be!
Home is where you are free, and when guests come
they have to except you as you are . . . at least it
should be!

Sister and Brother Love

Being little ones together is very comforting
You have a playmate
You have someone to pretend with
And as you get older
You have someone to protect or defend.
You fight
And sometimes you can really get on each other's
nerves
First you don't want them in your room
Unless you invite them in
You don't want them messing with your things
Or wearing your clothes
You beat them
Or they beat you, to the last piece of cake,
And they drink up what is left of the milk.
You can't like their friends
And you can't hang out with them either
Then,
When they get angry at you,
They tell your secrets
And they become your enemy.
Sometimes
You wish you weren't related.
You accept the fact that you resemble each other
Your hands and feet are shaped the same way.

As you grow older,
You learn to like them, for you have so much in
common
And
You begin to appreciate them.
You're even proud of them
You hang out and admire your kinship
You look forward to seeing them and spending time
together.
You become protective,
Selective when they start dating.
Cool or not
You let them know how you feel about their choices.
You have a desire
To want to be included in their lives
Forever
(Oh what a bond)
How great it is to have a brother,
A sister
And share roots
You know them
You love them
They are bone of your bone
And same blood running through your veins
Why not?
That sister, brother love
Is amazing!

Daddy's Chair

I remember skipping down 18th street.
I was going to see my Daddy, oh what a treat
Heading for the Barber Shop,
Some say it was the hot spot.
I would go there
Climb up in my Daddy's Chair.
So see
He would pretend to cut my hair.
He would pin that big apron on me
I was footloose and fancy free
Just thinking about what my Daddy did for me
In my Daddy's Chair
He would pretend to cut my hair
The guy in the other chair would say
"Hey is that your daughter?"
Daddy would say "Yeah"
And he'd give me a quarter.
My Daddy would tell joke after joke
When he finished, he'd buy me a coke.
After sitting in Daddy's Chair
Where he would pretend to cut my hair

My Daddy did many other wonderful things for me.
But I especially recall my visits to his shop
Where I'd sit in his number one chair
And he would pretend to cut my hair.
He would call my mother on the phone.
He would say "Girl,"
(That's what affectionately called her),
"She on her way home."
After a hug and a kiss
This treat I would never miss
Our time together.
What he did for me.
Oh! Little girl memories are precious and sweet
For my Daddy was awesome and he was unique.
Oh I have since
Longed to be there
In my Daddy's Chair
Where for me he would pretend to cut my hair!

-Thank you Daddy

My Mama's Hands

My mama was a member of the ways and means,
And with her hands, she did all sorts of things.
She had mending hands,
Molding hands and "Ouch!"-
She had scolding hands.
Those hands could bake,
Some, "Sure you right," delicious pies and cakes
Cuttin' greens and snappin' beans
Preparin' squash
O' good gosh!
Why, the only time I saw that hand ball up into a fist
Is when you brought the wrong thing on her grocery
list.
Fixin' hands,
Mixin' hands,
If you couldn't do it,
Those were some lead me to it hands
Now, around my house,
If you got sick
Here comes Mama
And in her hands was the bottle of "Father John's"
Or that blue jar of Vick's
She, many of times
Would make some down home recipe
Made it special for what is ailing my family and me.
Those hands could also crochet and knit,

Folks would say
"Take it in. Let it out. Can you hem it? Trim it? O'
it's too tight!
Those hands were busy.
Stayed up a many a night
Those hands could make
Choir robes, Pastor Capes, wedding gowns and
window drapes.
Now down the street,
Lived the Stevens, the Alexanders, the Smiths and
the Creeds
They placed in my Mama's hands
All their household keys.
Honey, with brown paper bag
My Mama would roll my hair!
Why I was the black Shirley Temple,
I had curls everywhere.
My Mama made lovin' my Daddy such an unique
passion art,
I saw that love,
I saw it flowing from her heart.
Sharing hands
Daring hands
Lord knows she had praying hands
But then, one day,
My Mama's hands turned to wings.

I lost my Mama,
And my Daddy lost his Queen!
People told me that God knows best
I guess those hands were tired and they needed rest.

But, when I became a mother
And looked into my son's eyes
And touched his gentle face.
I could close my eyes and feel my Mama's warm
embrace
So all you seniors,
You little ones'
And you teens,
Don't ever forget about the ways and the means
I shall never ever forget about the love and nurturing
Of my Mama's Hands.
I miss you Mommy.

Thank you!

Grandma's Blues

Her name was Mercy Murtle Anna Laura Lula Maxey. Some called her "Mother Maxey" "Ain't Mert" and "Sista." But me, I was so very fortune because I called her one of the greatest names. I called her Grandma. A woman short in statue, but tall in character. Now, at a very early age I discovered some news. This fine lady had "Grandma's Blues." She be up stairs in her room, sitting in her "Grandma Chair" handling her grandma business, crocheting or sewing and hummin. Oh that hummin used to get on my nerves. See, I would be in my room playing with my Barbie dolls, and sometimes Ken. And I couldn't hear me talkin, for all that ol' noise coming from the next room.

Well one day, I heard Grandma in her room singin and talkin real loud. So I went to the door of her room and I asked Grandma a question, not being disrespectful cause that was not wise, oh no! Not in our home! I asked, grandma, "Who you talkin' to?" She looked up at me and had a very assuring look on her face, content, like she was enjoying herself. And she said to me, "Pumpkin," as I was affectionately called, "I'm talking to Jesus!" I said "Jesus?! You talkin' to Jesus?" I looked around the room, and I didn't see Jesus. All I saw was Thelma Lou and Betty Olivebell, Grandma's dolls that were on her bed, placed in a lying down position with porcelin faces and red cheeks. They had big eyes that seemed to follow you wherever you went in Grandma's room. Grandma said, "Pumpkin, you know God reveals things to you and that Devil will show you the rest. You just keep living Baby, and whatever you undertake in life to do, do your best. Live right, live clean and treat your life like it's a gift that you are so very glad to have." I tried to understand Grandma but I was so confused. She was always sayin things that were for me a little hard to understand. So I went to my momma and I told her that I had some news. I said, "I think grandma's got the blues". Well momma was acting and looking like she knew what I was talking about. How could this be when I didn't really know? In any case momma started asking me some questions. She said, "Pumpkin, you ever think grandma might be thinking about your grandpa?" I thought, well, that could be it, the reason grandma seemed strange. Maybe she's missing her brother and sisters. And I thought, well she did have a lot of them. Uncle Will, Uncle Bill, Auntie Bama and Aunt Mert. Who knows? Then my momma said something I never thought I would ever hear. She said to me, "Pumpkin, ever think that grandma is missing her mother?" "Why, Grandma had a mother", I replied. Grandma has been old all of my life. Then I began to realize that grandma had to be a little girl at some point and time in her life. My momma said if I pay attention life will take me some places I will have never found on my own. Well, as time went on, grandma was three months from turning one hundred years old before making her transition. Before this, she would often sing, "I'm trying to make one hundred cause ninety nine and a half won't do". Later on in my life I grew up and my momma grew older. One evening I went to my momma's for a visit. As I walked up the stairs and down the hallway, I heard a familiar sound. I heard moaning, singing, and even laughter. I peeped through the banister and at that very moment I discovered something. My momma had grandma's blues. Oh my! I went into the room and asked my momma if she was alright. She said she was doing fine. She said she was just thanking God for everything he done for her. Then she told me that whatever I do, do it well. After a while I had my own child. I grew older and my momma made her transition too. One day I was sitting in my room sewing a letter on my son's jacket, and I began thinking about when he was little and how God kept him from all danger. He kept his mind and body, and I thought of how many times he made me proud to be his momma. I started to sing and hum and moan, and I was really into it. When I opened my eyes, my son was right there looking at me, and he and I both had realized that I too had caught it. I done caught grandma's blues. But you know what? It ain't so bad. I understand that my grandma and my momma was happy and not sad. I told my son to do his best and live good because God would bless him. Oh I remember so many things and right there I said, "Thank you grandma, thank you momma. I love and I miss you both". I then began to sing "Remember Me, remember me". So just know that as you live, you too will find out some news. You just might get GRANDMA'S BLUES!!

Pop-Pop
Was A Good Man

Pop-pop was a good man
And a lot of fun
He told me stories
We colored pictures
We even had pillow fights

Pop-pop told jokes
And laughed real hard
Pop-pop smelled good too!
Pop-pop was a very good man!

He took me to the circus
And many other places!
We went for evening walks
And talked about the sky and the trees
He made me see the real beauty
Of nature and simple things

Pop-pop fed me and gave me good things to eat
He also brought me lots of toys
We went to Disney World
And rode lots of fast rides
Pop-pop liked fast rides and amusement parks.

Pop-pop was a good man
My daddy
My friend
My buddy
And <u>mine</u> alone.
But then, Pop-pop got sick
And I took care of him
I read him stories
And drew him pictures

I fed him good things to eat
Because you see,
My Pop-pop was a good man!
And he will forever be in my heart.

The New Baby

New life is coming soon into this world!
Parents often wonder, when is the baby coming?
Is it a boy or a girl?
Will it have it's daddy's eyes?
Or it's mother's nose?
Will it have all its fingers and cute little toes,
Will it be pretty or handsome?
Will her skin be fair?
Will his face be long or round?
Will her head be full of hair?
Will he roll, crawl, walk, and talk at his own pace?
Will she cry various cries to summon one to her space?
Will his food go down right?
And at the allotted time, will she sleep through the
night?
Will his bones and teeth develop?
Will they be strong?
Or will they be weak and show that something is
wrong?
Will she be a friendly or spoiled child?
Will her attitude be calm and her spirit mild?
Will he be a child that's caring and respected?
Or will he be the outcast one who is teased and
rejected?
Will he know wrong from right?
Or will he be a child who likes to argue, fuss and fight?

Will he like to go camping or on a hike?
Will he enjoy the outdoors, will he ride a bike?
Can she make friends, can she be trusted on her own
or will he rather not be bothered and want to be left
alone?
Will he be honest, kind hearted and true?
Or will he be a liar, whose goal is to fool you?

Will she be able to make it through trouble, struggles
and strife?
Or will he be wandering through without a goal or
dream in life?
When school day comes, will he pay attention?
Will she be good in class?
Will she be a fast learner or will he barely pass?
Will he listen to his teacher and a lengthy time sit
down?
Or when the teacher's teaching will he act like a
clown?
When he plays
Will he wear a vindictive frown or smile?
Will someone ever say?
"My, what a pleasant child."
Will he appreciate the opportunity to go to school?
Or, will he go astray down some dark path and mostly
break the rules?

Will she want to go to college?
Or claim to have all the answers
All the knowledge?
Well lord,
Yes we wonder
And we are worried,
Because we don't know what to expect!
God answered and laid on their hearts,
Have I ever failed you yet!
You need not worry but fall on your knees,
And never forget to pray.
For, I will direct,
I will guide,
And keep him day to day.
Don't you fret and don't doubt I've got your corner
So don't waste time figuring things out.
When the new baby comes,
Whether a boy or girl,
I've not only created that life, but
I created the entire world!

My Man Child

There was one, who came before you,
But with me he could not stay,
I cried sad tears and grieved a lot day after day.
But Man child,
I sought the face of God and I began to pray,
Lord,
I want a child of my own.
Little did I know?
You were on your way.
I remember the day we met,
I looked into those hazel green eyes,
For you were my much wanted miracle,
Not an "Oops" or sudden surprise.
So, I asked God,
Show me this parent thing!
I don't know what to do!
God said'
"Love, guide, and nurture him
But,
Let me see him through you!
I watched you play with "Ninja Turtles"
Walking around in your pop pops shoes
"Power Rangers" and "Transformers,"
Oh, how you loved to watch the News.

Can't forget about your dinosaurs,
Triceratops and T-Rex
Your love for bees, bugs, plants and ants,
My word, what will be next.
Why you wanted to bring home a snake, a chameleon,
or some creepy thing from the sea.
You said,
"Mom can I bring it home?"
I said,
"Huh? Not to live with me!"
You taught yourself how to ride a bike, swim and
rollerblade.
It's true!
Your mom couldn't master those things,
So Man-child,
Good for you.
Love always found time to read a book
You learned to sew and even cooked.
You were fond of traveling,
I made sure you did.
You've been many places,
And you shared with me the information learned
And your views of cultures and races.

Now,
Your sophomore and junior years
You didn't make many mistakes
For you and I know, Man-child,
It was a blessing and not a lucky break.
Many have complemented me on your character
I told them
"My Man-child has set some goals, got some plans,
O' by the way,
I'm glad to say
He turned out to be a mighty fine young man."
So, as I look back,
I reminisce about these wonderful years.
We're here today and I'm proud to say,
I'm crying happy tears.

Getting Ready
For Sunday Morning Service

Getting ready for Sunday morning service at my
house was like a holiday
The smell of a big breakfast was in the air
The weather outside was kinda fair
Mama was up, after a long, sometimes sleepless night
Preparing our breakfast for us,
Just right.
Now, my eggs were scrambled well
And I think Daddy's too!
Mama's eggs were soft and runny
And Grandma's eggs, the side that was up, she called
it "Sunny."
We get partially dressed and head downstairs,
Sit in our assigned seats,
We had our own special chairs!
And as long as you were able to sit at the table.
Mama would say
"Daddy please say the blessing, for time is pressing."
We would eat, clean the kitchen and finish getting
dressed.
Mama said,
"Hurry up and don't leave a mess!"
Grandma would always beat us to it
For getting dressed, she didn't hesitate.

She was on the "Mothers' Board" and she hated
being late.
Daddy's walking around and asking
"What tie do you like best?"
Mama would say
"The one that's gray looks good on you with that
vest."
My Daddy would smile like a child.
My Mother was so sharp in her Sunday meeting
attire
To dress like her when I got grown,
Was one of my desires.
Her perfumed smelled up the room.
I'd be in the bathroom looking in the mirror
Daddy would say
"Sing good!"
For he gave me confidence
I knew I would.
We'd be singing with the radio
Our voices bouncing from wall to wall ceiling to the
floor.
Thanking and praising God as we walked out the
door.
Something about this Sunday morning story and my
family and me.

To God be the Glory

Aunt Mollie's Years

I have an Aunt named Mollie,
Who was born on the 4th of July
She is so special
Here are the reasons why
Aunt Mollie is a hundred and two
With good memory, good humor and good vision,
There's a lot Aunt Mollie can do!
She's spry, informative, and still does her chores
Especially her gardening
And she loves the outdoors
She's grown pacemmon, strawberries, melons and
chickpeas
Along with okra, pecans
Did I mention pear trees?
Aunt Mollie has lived through 21 Presidents
And the Great Depression
She roared with the twenties
And said "Now, that's a discussion!"
The invention of airplanes, radio, and television.
War time, peace time and a time of prohibition.
Military changes,
A man walking on the Moon
The mistreatment of minorities
When equal rights seemed doomed.

She witnessed the civil rights movement
And the work of Dr. Martin King
His marching,
In hopes this nation would let Freedom ring
She saw the change in automobiles,
Balloons with hot air,
She traveled to New York to see the World's Fair
What amazed Aunt Mollie is the computer and the
cell phone
People can talk all they want
And don't have to be home.
Aunt Mollie says
"Folks ask, how have you lived so long?"
Aunt Mollie said
"Well, I tell you the truth! I love God, I was obedient
and I tried to live right in my youth!
Yes, I've seen a lot, done a lot, been through a lot,
But my life is not a mystery.
If you think this is something,
Wait til' I turn a hundred and three!"

Healin' In The Kitchen

My mother loved to have company
Which was some female kinfolk.
There was Aunt Dora, Aunt Willie and Aunt
Rosetta
My Aunt Rose was my favorite
Also, there were some of my mother's sista friends
Ms. Ruth, Ms. Emma and Ms. Fannie
Now, I thought it very peculiar
That when the children of the house received
company
It was usually in the living room
Under the watchful eyes of an older sibling or adults.
Just to make sure that boys would be boys
And girls would remain girls.
Well, my mother would almost always escort or direct
her guest
Down the hall, through the dining room and into the
kitchen.
I was asked to serve my mother's
Freshly brewed iced tea
In the pretty glasses that I got out of the china closet
That we kids could not use
But we really didn't care
Because there was nothing like drinking a cold glass
of
Water, lemonade, or Kool-Aid

From a coffee, mayonnaise, or jelly jar.
Um! Um! Um!
Those ladies would pull up a chair around that table
Like they were gonna eat some of mother's good
nutritious food,
But instead, they wanted some food for thought.
They needed some healing in the kitchen.

One Aunt Dora stood up and declared,
"Times are hard, I can hardly pay my bills.
The road is rough when the battle is all up hill.
I feel like my life is a demolition,
So I pressed my way here to find healin',
Healin' in the kitchen"

Aunt Rosetta jumped up and belted out these words
"Sister, I know what you mean
I've been going through like you!
I fast pray and work hard!
I don't know what else to do.
I need to protest
With a "Help Me" petition
So I pressed my way here for some healin',
Healin' in the kitchen"

And there was Ms. Emma.
"Well, girls, in my house, the kids don't want to go to
school.

That man of mine, he's acting like a fool,
And my health is not in mint condition,
But I pressed my way for some healin',
Healin' in the kitchen.
There's nothing,
Absolutely nothing, like listening to those ladies.
All who seemed to be in the same position
Looking for healin there in the kitchen
Talkin', singin', prayin', and Healin'.

Sunday Night

There was no other night, like Sunday night.
Our family would assemble into the living room and
find a comfy spot on the sofa, chair, or floor.
Some of us kids would sit tight like ducks in a row
secretly fighting and hitting each other with our
elbows.
We would then sit patiently and wait for ice cream
and some of mama's homemade cake. We were ready
to watch the Wonderful World of Disney followed
by Ed Sullivan. Somebody would call and let my
parents know that somebody Black was on the show.
Now depending on who it was, we'd either be in tears
or up dancing.
But we did it together as a family, that's right.
There was no other night like Sunday night.

Family Reunion

Family reunion gathering is near
Meeting and greeting those so dear
Eating, singing, informing what's new
Taking group pictures of the entire crew!

Hey! Do you remember when . . . ?
Fond memories of the past
Oh, what feeling of kinship
I so want this time to last!

Remembering our bereaved seasons
We paused to shed a tear
Our patriarch and matriarch now gone
But in our hearts they will live on
His-story and Her-story is the essence of our being
That made us who we are

All my people here together
Some right here, some afar!
Adults and children growing older
For life continues to move on
New love
New marriages
Many babies being born

The games we've played
The races we've run
Laughter and cheering
Good clean fun!

Our family reunions are great but,
The most impressive thing I see
There is always someone in the midst
I find resembles me!
FAMILY!

They Say

Some people call me by name
Some just call me

They say,
My mother should not have given birth to me
My brothers
Or my sisters
They say,
My father is a danger to society
He does not have a strong mind
And can't follow their rules
(You know)

Never mind the sacrifices of my grandfather
The creative contributions of my grandmother
Never mind the free labor of my ancestors
Their many inventions
Their many firsts
And after all of that
They still don't know who I am

I'll show them
No, I'll tell them who I am
I am that unique piece to a puzzle
That cannot be completed without me.

Just For Me

People ask me what I want to be when I grow up, mainly adults. How dare they ask me that and they themselves are in a stalemate state of mind! I wonder what they did with the same opportunities. Drinking, smoking, doping, and not coping! Their life is sad and the worst thing that I can see as a youngster, is a grown up with a lightless life. No vision. No direction. No hope. No strength. They say one thing and do another. Sacrifice nothing but continue to be walking dead men and women taking up all the space. Think of all the people who would treasure their lives. But me; I will be different. You see, I have a plan and it will become a life of action. I refuse; I will not sit on this gift that the creator has provided "just for me—to share with others."

The Pastor

The Pastor has the most difficult job of minding our
Hearts, minds, and souls
He suggest we trust God's word
As our sinful life unfolds.
He introduces us to the productiveness of prayer
power.
He said
"People should pray often no matter the day, time, or
hour."
He teaches us how by example in loving, sharing, and
giving
And warns us all of a hardened heart.
A heart that's not meek or forgiving
He shows us how to study the Bible
And understand God's revelation
For it takes some ups and some downs to make
dedication
He instructs us how to apply the many lessons
learned
He reminds us of the many blessings
We have not always earned
So when you think you're losing it,
And heading for a disaster
Go to church and ask for him
For he is known as
THE PASTOR!

Message From a Slave Girl

Remember me?
I hope you do
I am the Earth's sun-kissed daughter
Out of slavery, I was not born but created
Your story lives in many of my life's trials and triumphs
I am the treasure of what was, is, and will be.

We sang in the field and while chopping wood
O' we sang of Freedom
And even death
Often times, death was better than captivity.
We clapped our hands
And stomped out feet
While running to the Freedom beat
We moan our pains
And our burdens light
So moan your blues
Sing your jazz
Speak your poetry
Preach your promises
But do make merry
Remember, remember
Where it all started,
Most of it anyway!

The Elders

The elders are like traffic signs and signals on this
road of life. They should be observed, acknowledged,
and respected for their place biblically, socially,
spiritually, and environmentally. They have done
much, seen much, and have known the highs and lows
in daily living. They are gifts with longevity. They can
guide and direct us if we are willing to let them. They
have raised villages, and they have nurtured many.
Like road signs, they bring to us a sense of order.
They sometimes demand us to slow down, get moving,
or just stand still wait and be patient. The elders or
seasoned ones are the true elite among our society.
Let's give them honor, quality time and attention.
You'll be wiser for doing so!

It's Not When You Start, But How You Finish

We live in a time of expectations, numerous
possibilities.
So much to do
So many responsibilities for some of us
Life may be rugged and may be rough
And we feel like it is too much
It's hard
But it's trouble that makes us tough
This life is a spiritual journey
With surprises and facts
Note:
It's just the weight you're carrying that puts a hump on
your back.
Keep on keepin' on
There may be some down falls,
But you make it,
Don't stop but stand tall
And dream your dreams
Never let them diminish!
Because,
It's not when you start
But,
It's how you finish.
Get ready, get set, Live!

Sista Friends

We've been close for many years
We laughed and cried many tears
Yes, often time you have been there
And my woes you are quite aware,
So, I appreciate you Girl!
For the countless things you do
However my darling, darling Sista
You got some woes too!

You like to point a finger and talk behind my back.
We've both said some hurtful things.
Is this how friends should act?
Now, I hope you want to keep us, my desire is that
you should.
But just in case you
DON'T, oops I misunderstood!

Don't Forget To Pray

From the moment you wake up,
And think of things to do today,
Before you leave your dwelling place,
Don't forget to pray!

There will be challenges you must face,
And face without delay,
In all of your decision making,
Don't forget to pray!

If you're criticized by some,
For what you do or say,
In your heart you know you're right,
Just don't forget to pray!

Many goals you have achieved,
Others are well on their way,
Be jubilant but focused,
And don't forget to pray!

Your desire to leave some places,
Some places you wish to stay,
Or could be what you need,
My friend, don't forget to pray!

You will not always win your battles,
And if you don't, it's okay,
Think of it as a lesson learned,
Don't forget to pray!

When you count all your blessings,
And gratitude you display,
You remember when, once again,
You took time to pray!

Change

You know,
There's a lot of people who's always hatin'
It's down right aggravating'
They find no jubilation
When a person makes a change.
So called friends try to rule you,
And get angry 'cause they can't fool you.
They have the nerve to say
"You are acting strange,"
It's change!
Darn, get used to it.
You may very well one day have to.
They see you in all of your glory,
But they don't know your story
Question
Why do folks dread when you try to better yourself,
and get ahead?
Just think,
If change was not discussed
We may very well find ourselves
Still sittin' in the back of the bus.
If change was not needed,
We would still tell our children

That they can grow up to be a doctor, lawyer,
preacher, teacher, or something with some upright
citizen intent,
But never, ever imagine that they could be
President!
Change!
Change allows us to dream our dreams,
Set our goals,
Know and own our rights,
Live our lives to the fullest potential!
Change is not odd.
Change is not a façade.
My friends,
Change is inevitable!

Life
Is More than Just Words

Life will take you through some ups and downs
Inside outs, and some turn arounds
You gotta keep striving; it's not over yet,
Sometimes what you see is not what you get
So hold on to the good times that you've had,
Hey! Come on now, it ain't been so bad,
So in case you think, "Oh how absurd"
Know that life is more
More than just words
It's more . . . . so much more than a word or two
It's more
It's not what you say, but it's what you do
Remember the story about the tortoise and the hare,
He didn't say (your faster than me)
THAT'S NOT FAIR
He took the challenge and kept a steady pace
Now you and I know who won the race
Cause it's more, so much more than
A word or two
It's more
It's not what you say, but it's what you do
It's more than a notion
There's no magic potion
So no matter what you've heard
Life is more
So much more
Than just words.

Miss Loosey

What I got ain't no surprise. They see my hips, my sexy lips and never look into my eyes. They wished they looked as good as I do. Sisters always hatin' while they men folk evaluating what's between my thighs. I love to show-n-tell and sometimes share. I cut to the chase, no I'm not ashamed cause' it's all a game. All those old ladies say I'm a disgrace. You see, I can be a man's baby cause a lot of men want more from a woman than a sweet little lady. They like it when we sexy girls strut our stuff. I give exactly what they want. They just can't get enough. A lot of men always sneakin' and flirtin' with me, because to them I am a mystery. Men hate women that talk too much, and I can be as quiet as a mouse, but my mama said I'll never get invited to their mothers' house. I got to change my ways. Maybe I need to wear something different, something not so revealing. Yeah, I try to wear something that's modest and appealing. So, I finish school and practice good morals and seek not a man, but knowledge and I try my best. I can go to college, and I might meet a very nice guy who likes me for me. They'll look past my physical parts and seek to know what's inside my heart, and I will be free!

Them Strange Men Folk

By: Micki Barocca and Sylvia Towns

There is a saying, "Let a woman be a woman
And let a man be a man"
But I tell you, them men folk just don't understand
They say we women complain too much
We nag and trip and do nothing but cause a fuss
But sometimes they make you wonder who wears the
pants
When they start leaving all the manly things to us

And some of them men folk don't even have a job
And if they do
They don't want to give up the money
But always want us to give up the honey,
and got the nerve to say we actin' funny

and still after all that we do
we gotta be their beauty queens
making sure that everything is in the same place like we
still in our teens
but he can walk around with his stomach hanging down
to your knees please

and how about the ones who
see all of your faults
but he's perfect in his own eyes
"oh, please brotha be advised
there is nothing permanent about a disguise"

most of us good women try to make a happy home
but some of them men folk can't help themselves
they got roaming in their bones
out in the streets and the bars and the clubs
looking for lust
because they don't have a clue about love

then you got those Godly men
who pretend that they are living right
Dr. Jekyll in the daytime
And Mr. Hyde at night

But they must have forgotten who designed us
For we are wonderfully and marvelously made
God birthed us from the rib in your side
And made us wonderful
And yes God also made us beautiful
Because men were not meant to be alone
But still yet, he must be worthy to occupy a throne

Ladies you know these words are true
And relationships ain't no joke
So all my good women we dedicate this one to you
so you can watch out for all them strange men folk!

Ain't No Way!

You can't love me and hate me at the same time
Ain't No way!

You can't neglect me
Disrespect me
And tell your friends and family
I'm your lady! No Baby!
Ain't No way!

So you want to make love to me today
But tomorrow
I feel you will make my blue skies the darkest gray!
Ain't No way!

You often act like you're leaving
Which proves your love is deceiving
And your actions are unbelieving
Ain't No way!

You make accusations
Of my involvement with men and women
And to my dismay
You asked was I gay!
Well
If that were true
What does it say about your manhood and you?
Don't play!
Ain't No way!

You always, always find fault
And say the meanest things
Don't you know?
Words hurt, bite, and sting
And you say you're my ever lovin' man!
Ain't No way!

Your mood changes more than the climate
When it's mixed up in seasons
You complain about the dumbest things,
For the dumbest reasons
You think you are perfect
Ain't No way!

You don't want to pay the cost
But you're the master at acting like you are the boss.
Honey
If this pertains to you . . .
Listen . . .
Step up,
Take charge,
Love us,
Respect us,
Be a God head man.

But if this task is too great
And being faithful is not in your plan . . .
We understand . . .
THAT IT AIN'T NO WAY!

O King

You said I've lost my status of being acknowledged as
your queen,
Yet you're *Majesty*,
You're a wanna be,
Only disguised as a king!
For a king
Loves, honors, and protects,
It's his duty to do things right.
FOR HE GUIDES AND GUARDS HIS
KINGDOM
WITH HIS POWER AND HIS MIGHT!
A TRUE KING NEVER ABANDONS
HIS QUEEN AND HIS THRONE,
MANY TIMES NOT PHYSICALLY
PRESENT,
HIS QUEEN IS NEVER LEFT ALONE.
HE ATTEMPTS TO DO HIS BEST,
AND SERVES UNTIL HE DIES OUT.
YOU'RE *Highness*,

You lack steadfastness,
It's without a shadow of doubt.
You have faltered in character both here and there
Especially with those whom should love you most.
Seems
You're not honored anywhere.
Sire
You said I lost my queen status and I can be replace,
The record of your life will show,
You're a king who has
Fallen
From
Grace!

To my friend

I'm the stranger that's within

There are some things I wouldn't share

For sometimes I wouldn't dare,

But you messing up and it isn't fair, so there.

You really need to listen

It's not always the smiles that glisten.

But to be real is the deal.

Don't let others steal that thing you call joy, please.

And with ease

Just try to do your best.

Try to pursue true happiness.

Mr. D (Deceitful)
Male Not Man

When Mr. D meets a good woman,
He's got a sad story to tell,
He masks his ratchet cunningness and wears it very
well!
He knows exactly what to say, and the right little
deeds he'll do.
For he schemes and gives you heartfelt dreams
To get up close to you!

That male is so unfaithful,
But to you he will often sing
"Oh baby I love and care for you"
But his words don't mean a thing!
Smelling good
From the hood
But don't believe he's for real
For loving, sharing, and caring
Was not part of the deal?
How can a man
Bad mouth his own family and friends
Of what they got
Or what they're not, yet
He lacks a window and a pot!

He views a family man as tied down
You see his life is a circus
He likes to clown around.
He bashes a man, who is dedicated to his woman,
To his wife,
Cause he needs several women
To fulfill his perverted empty life!
He knows you function at 100
While he functions at 35, because his character seems
so small,
When standing by your side!
He's not at all handsome
His words really aren't that sweet
Although, he looks like Mr. Big Guy
He's actually very weak!

He is actually Mr. Deceitful
Only Male, and not a Man!

Author's Bio

Mama Syl'V (AKA Sylvia Towns), Philadelphia native has a natural gift of storytelling. Her poems capture the soul as Mama invites the listener to walk down their own memory lane. She attended Cheyney (State) University and Temple University and graduated in 1982 under social administration with a degree in early childhood education.

Mama Syl'V has written and produced several of her own plays, "The World is a Stage of Entertainment" and "It's More Than Just Words" which inspired her to share her poetry. Mama Syl'V is currently working on her second and third books, "Have You Ever Seen a Two Legged Dog?" and "A Third Choice and Choices."

Her love for children and the performing arts has allowed her to produce a number of plays and stage productions over the years, which involve children of all ages. Many of her stage productions have premiered at Philadelphia's own Clef Club of Jazz and Performing Arts. She currently works for Universal Companies as a L.I.M.A. (Librarian) and continues to teach and inspire her students to be creative by helping them to enhance their own creativity.

She has a media team, a book club and a performing arts club. Sylvia has one son, Vaughn and eight siblings.

Stay tuned . . .

Acknowledgements

To God be the glory, for all the blessings he sends my way. I want to thank my brother, **Kala Jojo**, for his encouragement and support, and for showing me that through his gift, that I had gifts also. He helped me to challenge myself to bring them forth and to be grateful for our roots.